How I Got My Son Back

A man's journey to fatherhood

GLENN P BROOKS, JR.

How I Got My Son Back

A man's journey to fatherhood

Glenn P Brooks, Jr.

Copyright © 2014

All rights reserved.

No part of this publication may be reproduced, stored in a retrieval system, or transmitted, in any form or by any means – electronic, mechanical, photocopying, recorded, or otherwise – without prior written permission.

ISBN: 1499584113

ISBN-13: 978-1499584110

Printed in the United States of America

Cover design by Vexed Graphics

To my son, Justin

When you came into my life almost 21 years ago I never had any intention of leaving you, but because of my own selfishness I did and for that I'm sorry.

You deserved to have me in your life full time. For all the times that I wasn't there and for all the moments that I missed, I'm so grateful that I had an opportunity to make things right.

Son I am so proud of how you have turned out to be a very respectful and forgiving young man. Thank you for forgiving me and for allowing me back into your life. Even though we had our rough patches your love for me and your desire to have me in your life motivated me to do the right thing. We are still growing and I look forward to seeing our relationship continue to grow over the years.

It's not over this is just the beginning!

CONTENTS

	Introduction	vii
1	No Clue	11
2	Living Single	29
3	My Fault	37
4	MAN UP! Accept Responsibility	43
5	Fathering From Afar	51
6	No More Baby Mama Drama	65
7	Be Careful What You Ask For…	75
8	Mending Broken Pieces	89

INTRODUCTION

My experience growing up in a single parent home and without a father really put me in a perfect position to understand how that feels and how it can affect kids. Today I've committed my life to growing and changing. I wrote this book after a friend of mine, Deron Cloud encouraged me to share with people the story of "How I got my son back".

This book is written to fathers who want to be involved in the lives of their sons but are separated from them. That separation could be as a result of divorce, separation, or from a relationship that is no longer intact for whatever reason. I am going to share my story with you and what I did about the one thing I could control or influence … and that was ME. Every story is unique, my experience may be different from yours but there are some basic truths that I believe are universal.

1. Accept your reality…it is what it is.
2. Look for a solution
3. Always keep the main thing, the main thing.
   (it is ALWAYS about your child's needs)
4. Understand what true humility looks like
5. No matter what…Show Love

I don't believe that you can change anyone but yourself. However when you change, people tend to change in their response toward you. I lost my son because of my selfishness and hopefully through my story you can find the strength to tell yourself the "brutal truth". Once you do that, change is possible. It doesn't guarantee that you'll get back what you lost, but it does mean that your soul, (your mind, will and emotions) can be healed. Therefore the quality of your relationships will take on new meaning which could ultimately position you for a second chance.

GLENN P. BROOKS, JR.

Chapter 1

No Clue

When I was a child, I talked like a child, I thought like child, I reasoned like a child. When I became a man, I put the ways of childhood behind me.
1 Corinthians 13: 11

I remember it like it was yesterday, my mother kept asking me why? Is she pregnant? No ma she's not pregnant, we just want to get married. But son she's only 19 and your just 20, you guys have plenty of time, what's the rush? She'd ask over and over again. The only answer I could give was that "we were in love" and we just want to take it to the next level. The real deal was that we were having sex like rabbits and as a Christian I knew that having sex outside of marriage was going against what the Bible taught.

It never dawned on me that we were missing something. That we were using sex to actually medicate or fill a void that was created by our circumstances or how we grew up. I didn't know anything about me at the time, I didn't know who I was, what I wanted, where I was going, or how I was going to get there, and neither did she. All we knew was that when we were together it felt good, and it felt right. We didn't know we were going about it the wrong way. We were like two kids in a candy store. We wanted what we wanted and we had to have it right now. So we did what most young immature hormonal kids do and we pushed all the practical wisdom and good advice to the side, labeled it "they're just trying to run our lives". Today that would sound like "why is everybody hating on us?" Whatever you want to call it, at the end of the day we got exactly what we wanted. We said "I DO".

Things were fine for the first year or so. We even came to a conclusion that we were young and didn't have to have any children until later. We decided to wait, by using birth control for five years before trying to get pregnant. We stuck to that goal, but what we didn't do was grow together, we actually grew apart. I thought marriage meant I could have sex as much as I wanted and whenever I wanted. No one had ever taught me how to consider my wife or what she wanted. More importantly no one had modeled for me how to be "the man". When I say "the man" I mean more than just physically being a male but being a man that she could respect, love, and even follow. I was not a man of character or integrity. I didn't know that I was supposed to become a better person through growth. I didn't know how to discipline my mind and body to do what needed to be done. Instead I did what I knew to do, and that was, to do "me".

Before we go any further you need to understand that I didn't grow up with an example of what a "real relationship" with a woman looked like. Having been exposed to pornography at a very early age I had learned that girls or women were something simply for the pleasure of men. Although we had known each other as kids we grew up in very different environments. My example of relationships came from my parents. They were divorced when I was 6 and my mom did the job of both parents. She was constantly working trying to make ends meet because my father wasn't paying any child support. My father on the other hand got to live his life and do as he pleased showing up when he felt like it but never consistently.

Remember children watch what you do and usually end up imitating your actions whether good, bad, or indifferent.

As I look back now I truly appreciate that she did the best she knew and for that I'm grateful. The absence of a devoted father only fueled my becoming a rather crafty manipulator. I had most people fooled for most of my childhood. I was becoming more and more selfish and did whatever it took to get what I wanted. I got caught plenty of the time doing things I had no business doing. Things like stealing, getting high and having sex all before the age of 12. On the occasions when I did get caught with "my hand in the cookie jar" I would adamantly deny it and do my best to persuade my mom she didn't see what she saw. When she wasn't convinced she would do all she could which was to beat me. In time the pain from the beating would wear off and I would keep doing what I wanted with even more determination to get better at it so I wouldn't get caught. I rarely experienced any serious consequences for my actions and I now know that "getting away" with the crazy stuff I did really hurt me later. It served to mold me into a man who was extremely "self-centered" and "self-serving".

After years of mastering how to get my way I got involved with the woman who would eventually be the mother of my son. She was raised in a situation that was the polar opposite of mine. She had both parents in the house and from the outside looking in they seemed to have it all. She lived in a house in the country with a little land and her parents were very much involved in her day to day life. I remember when we started dating "we all dated" her mom, her dad and me. They wouldn't allow her out of their sight with me. A date consisted of going over to her house, talking with her and her parents while sitting in the basement family room watching a movie on TV, or maybe a video and eating pizza or ice cream and cake.

Sounds like a really nice evening doesn't it? That is a nice evening for the first date, but after a few months of that exact same routine, trust me I was bored. I remember asking her "Why are your parents always around? We need to go out by ourselves. I'm bored with doing the same stuff over and over again, ain't you?" I'd say. Her response was something to the effect of "yeah I would love to do something different but they never let me do anything".

Now you have to remember that by this time I've been at this game of getting over on people with my charm for a couple of years and every time I got away with it I grew more confident. I never had a problem mustering up enough courage to ask for what I wanted, maybe not directly but indirectly. I remember approaching her father and asking would it be ok if we went to the movies together. I'll never forget his response "Oh son, we got plenty of movies… why would you need to go out?" It was clear that they were not about to let their baby girl out of their sight. This only fueled my desire to get my way and caused me to come up with a plan to get her alone. As time went by and I played it cool they eventually started loosening their grip on her. They eventually grew comfortable with the idea of letting her ride with me for a quick errand or something. But that wasn't nearly enough for me. If you gave me an inch, trust me I was gonna get more out of the deal.

By now I was a senior in high school, had a job, which meant I had my own money, and access to use my mother's car as much as I wanted. I was on a partial schedule, which meant I only had three classes, so every day I was out of school by 11:30 am. Back then you were considered "the man" if you had this much freedom. So I started "dropping seeds" with her about me picking her up from school early. After some careful planning that day had finally arrived. We planned that she would go to the school nurse complaining of a stomach ache, and wanted to call her "brother" to get her from school. We didn't have cell phones in 1984, so we had to carefully coordinate the whole thing. We planned that at a certain time she would go to the office with this fake story and after an agreed amount of time I'd simply show up. I went to the nurse's office and told her I had come to pick up my sister who was sick, she simply signed her out and we were on our way. There was "No ID required" back then and nobody was thinking about kids skipping school or being snatched like they are today. When I think about it, kids today have to come up with much more elaborate plans to get away with some of the things I got away with back then. At any rate we now had about 3 hours to do whatever we wanted before she had to be back in time to ride the bus home from school so no one would be the wiser. We did this several times without the school or her parents ever knowing what was up. These secret trips set the stage for us to eventually have sex and losing her virginity. She was a willing participant but she had no idea that I had been quietly persuading her and manipulating her to go to the next level in our relationship. It was terrible but I had set out to do what I wanted and to get her to be ok with it, after all we were "going together" and that's what you did. Eventually her parents found out months later and by that time I had this girl pretty much willing to do anything I asked. Now in all honesty, back then I didn't see that I was "playing games" with her, I was doing what I thought you were supposed to do. I thought I was a "grown man" by doing "grown" things like having a job and a girlfriend. I was a young boy with selfish ambitions, but because I didn't have much accountability or checks and balances, I was pretty much left to myself. Thinking back, this was innocent on the surface, however, when one thing quickly led to another before I knew it I had a bunch of people really angry with me including my girlfriend. After a major falling out with her parents, I was forbidden from ever speaking to her again, much less see her. We were both still minors, so if her parents really stuck to their guns, it made having a relationship almost impossible. I graduated later that year and started working full-time and she went on with her life. I attempted to connect with her but it was just too difficult with her folks totally against it.

A year or so later I went into the army and she enrolled in college. We hadn't been in touch with each other for a year and half and were moving on with our lives. Then one day I got a letter from her while I was in basic training. I can't remember what it said, but I will never forget how it started. "If you still care for me half as much as I care for you." Needless to say I was intrigued. I had pretty much moved on emotionally and had no idea that this woman was still interested. I responded to her letter and soon we were writing back and forth and eventually talked on the phone. It did not take long for the emotional and physical desire to be together to return. Things were becoming serious and I started making plans so I could see her when I got home from basic training. We struck up the relationship pretty much where it had left off – this time NO PARENTS. Shortly after graduating from basic training I found out that I would be stationed in New Jersey, which was just a little over two hours away from home and roughly three hours away from her college. It was crazy, everything was working out perfectly, we were young and in love. I would go to her school every single weekend for months until eventually we decided to get married.

Earlier I mentioned that *children watch what you do and usually end up imitating your actions whether good, bad, or indifferent.* Growing up without a father to model man-hood, leaves a void and most fill that void with the first thing or person that comes along that show's interest. For me that void was filled by the affection of a woman. I raised myself without the guidance of a father so through trial and error I had to figure it out. The challenge with that was that I was getting "on the job" training with real lives and real situations, so needless to say I was destroying people's lives in the process.

Our marriage was doomed from the beginning, we

got married for the wrong reasons and because we thought we were grown we didn't listen to anyone who tried to persuade us to wait. The honeymoon phase ended rather quickly and our marriage began to self-destruct almost immediately. I caused major damage in the first four years of our marriage that we would eventually realize could not be repaired. She had no idea that I had betrayed her trust about two years into our marriage with an emotional affair in the months prior to my discharge from the military. This emotional disconnect led to my second affair which would be a physical and sexual affair with an old girlfriend. I remember feeling terrible and walking around with this guilty conscious for months. The guilt grew to be too much and I couldn't take it anymore and I finally broke down and told her. Needless to say it shattered her, she had no idea of what I was capable of at the time. Once she got over the initial shock and pain we decided that we wanted to figure out how to get past this. After all I was sorry and I promised to never do it again. We decided to go to our pastor for guidance. We sat with our pastor for hours sharing our feelings, crying and praying. By the time we left I remember thinking "that's it, I confessed and it's over".

Well I wish I could say that we lived happily ever after. Instead of the story ending there, it really just got started. What I didn't know then that I know now is that when you go through a traumatic experience like that prayer alone doesn't change things. In order for real change to happen there are real things "actions" that need to be made. For there to be real change boundaries need to be erected to insure that you don't keep doing the same thing over and over again. Unfortunately for us this never happened and over the next eight to ten years I'd have many more affairs some emotional, some physical but nevertheless these acts of selfishness would be the foundation of a failed relationship. Let me repeat this, when you've never been taught what right looks like and how to achieve that, it's inevitable that you'll stumble through life trying to figure it out. Take it from me; this is a vicious cycle that leaves a wake of hurt people and damaged relationships. After you experience enough rejection, feelings of hopelessness begin to set in. That's when most people throw their hands up and begin to accept the all too famous saying "this is just who I am". When the truth is "it's not who you are, it's who you've become".

GLENN P. BROOKS, JR.

Chapter 2
Living Single

Being in a relationship with a single mindset never works, it never has and it never will.

Over the years I have met so many brothers who have the same "mindset" that I had when I got married the first time. That mindset was, although I am married I intend to live a life free of accountability as if I were still "single". Having been there before I understand, *when you don't have a model or a plan to follow, you'll make one up*. I remember not wanting to accept the fact that I was no longer single, I couldn't come and go or just do what I wanted without considering what my wife wanted or even liked for that matter. I didn't understand that being married was more than just getting a "get booty, wherever and whenever you wanted it" card. When you're a single adult no body questions "where are you going?" or "when will you be back?" or "call me if you're going to be late for dinner." you only have to answer to you.

The challenge for me was that I had some very unrealistic expectations of what a marriage should be. **Remember when you don't have a model or a plan to follow, you'll make one up.** Oftentimes it will be based on what you've seen or picked up here in there, along the way. I've learned the hard way, that this is a recipe for disaster.

I was committed to my idea of marriage and I was

willing to do whatever to keep this idea alive. My idea of marriage was I had a fulltime girlfriend/wife who I could hang out with and have fun whenever I wanted to. We could talk all the time like we did when we were dating and things would be just like dating only we would be living together. She would be down with whatever I wanted to do and we would never have arguments. Basically I thought it would be an extension of us going together. It didn't take long for me to realize that my idea was unrealistic, she actually saw us being married as a total 100% commitment. She saw what she saw in her parents, that you could fuss and fight but never leave each other. Certainly that you would never consider stepping out on each other or betraying one another's trust. She had plans for our future and I was simply living in the moment. She went from being my girlfriend to being my wife and I was still being her boyfriend. Our being on totally different pages soon led to my developing a dislike for who she really was – a very responsible, forward thinking, settled person. This led me to start coming up with stories just to get out of the house. I would go out and then I wouldn't "return her pages" (telling my age now). I started keeping things from her, even if it was something that would affect us both. I had no regard for time, how much I took or how little I gave. It was all about me. If I was upset and didn't want to talk for days that's what I did. If I wanted to stay out late "working" that's what I did. As far as I was concerned I was grown and I could do what I wanted and when I wanted. This mindset is not only disrespectful, but it is steeped in selfishness and immaturity. That's how I could detach myself from what was "right" and do what I felt. I was a little boy in a man's body, and the crazy thing was that I would drag my first wife through this foolishness for years. She had no idea who she had really hooked up with and what kind of damage I was capable of inflicted on her, but neither did I at that time in my life.

The single mindset is just that. It is a single minded focus that serves you well when you are by yourself. It helps you survive, it causes you to pay attention to the things you need, and ultimately it serves to shape you. When you are single you have no one else to care for but you. The challenge is that when you find yourself in a relationship with a person this mindset no longer serves that purpose. Teamwork is when two people come together to accomplish one goal. Many of you have heard the phrase that there is no I in team. Well this applies in relationships just like it does to championship teams. Not knowing this then is where I failed my relationship with my first wife and my son the most. I failed to develop as a team player and I only focused on my individual wants, desires, and needs which ultimately ended in my team (my family) coming in last place.

Long before my son was born this idea of playing as an individual gave birth to my ability to detach from what was most important to the team. My inability to see that I needed to change in this area led to my growth in this unproductive way of thinking. When you are willing to overlook or ignore when those closest to you are showing you an area in your life that needs change, you are setting yourself up for failure. It is just a matter of time, when it will happen not if.

In my first book "How to Raise A Man…Not A

Mommas Boy" I dedicated an entire chapter to the topic of "Missing in Action". I talk about the devastating effects on a child when his father is "missing". The numbers of kids growing up in a single parent home are reaching epidemic proportions. Think about it. Mothers are being put in a situation to the do the job of both parents and unfortunately the children, which includes you and me, have and are still paying the price. My dad left me to myself and because of my immaturity and selfishness I did the same thing to my son. Fellas if this vicious cycle is going to change, it must begin with us.

GLENN P. BROOKS, JR.

Chapter 3

My Fault

*The first step to recovery is admitting that YOU have a problem.
When you blame you remain.*

Before I can tell you how I got my son back I have to tell you how I lost him. I could blame losing my marriage and ultimately my relationship with my son on a bunch of stuff (from my upbringing, to not having a father, to my many adulterous affairs) but the truth lies in ME. It was MY fault; I made a series of poor choices that led to poor behaviors that ultimately eroded what relationships I did have. My mother always told me and I found it to be true that whenever there is more than one person involved in something, when things go wrong it is rarely all one person's fault. This chapter will help you understand that in order to reclaim what you've lost; you first must develop the ability to be brutally honest with yourself. To the degree that you are willing to see what you see in yourself will determine your ability to change. Without your being totally honest with yourself your ability to reclaim what you have lost will always elude you.

Let me start by sharing with you some of my truths. From the very beginning of my marriage to my first wife my expectations were off. I had no intention on growing our relationship, just continuing it as it was when we were dating. I was ignorant and didn't know nor had I ever been exposed to what a real, positive, and functional marriage looked like. I would have had to have been willing to invest in the marriage and learn how to be a good husband and eventually a good father. Looking back on it now I needed some help. That is why today I can recommend to young brothers to slow down, take the time to learn who they are, where they want to go and how they plan to get there before committing to long term relationships. If I would have had the opportunity to do that I believe the outcome of my first marriage would have been different.

Five years into our marriage after my numerous affairs, my wife and I had a son. Sadly this new addition to our family did not change my behavior. I continued to do "me" and I left her to herself to raise our son while I continued to live "singly married". This went on until a few months after my son's second birthday. At this point my wife had finally had enough and she left me for good. I had all but single handedly destroyed my marriage. Make no mistake I was an arrogant, prideful, hypocritical jerk who was extremely selfish. Although most people didn't meet <u>that</u> guy initially. Just like my first wife most people met my personality then later got to know my character. It took us another three years before we would finally divorce but it wasn't until then that I'd begin to see how much damage I had caused.

My first wife was a sweet and loving person. She had her problems but she was reasonable and a very forgiving person. I stomped all over that, figuratively speaking. She became a bitter, non-trusting, spiteful and cold person dealing with me. It was only after separating and having to deal with her now as a single mother that caused me to see how bad I'd messed her up. After we separated I would pick my son up every other weekend and that was kind of weird; it allowed me the opportunity to see how what I had done had affected him and his mother. To be honest in order to convince myself that I was ok, I started telling myself that this was all her fault. I'd say stuff like, she should've been a better wife, a better friend, a nicer more spontaneous person, when the truth was she did the best she could with what she had to work with. I was feeling guilty, as I should've been. I learned long time ago that **whenever there is more than one person involved in something, when things go wrong its rarely all one person's fault.** If that's true, in my case our coming unglued was at least 85% my fault.

GLENN P. BROOKS, JR.

Chapter 4

MAN UP!!
Accept Responsibility

It took both of you to create this child, so why would you believe that it wouldn't take both of you to raise him.

I had screwed up, so I gave up and decided I didn't want to fight to do what was right. It was easier to stop trying. Yeah I grew up without a father but I also knew right from wrong. Finally it all came to me one Sunday morning while sitting in church almost two years after the final separation. I can't tell you the name of the message or even what my pastor was teaching but I distinctly remember him saying "you need to go back and apologize". It was like I was the only one in the room. It was like I heard God himself say Glenn, this drama that you're experiencing was caused by you and if you want it to end you must humble yourself and apologize. Now it wasn't like I heard God say this in an audible voice, it was a strong nudge that I felt in my gut. For years I'd been running from the truth and I couldn't take it anymore. I wanted to move on with my life and more than that I was ready to man up to the responsibility of being a real father.

Soon after coming to this conclusion I called my soon to be ex-wife and asked her to go to lunch with me so we could talk. There was no reason that she should have agreed to do that, by this time we only talked when we had to. I wasn't in trouble with the courts for not paying child support, we had a visitation schedule with my son that we agreed to and for the most part, kept up with. We were very close to filing for divorce and by all signs we were both moving on. However I needed to let her know something I should've said years ago.

If my memory serves me correctly we sat down at a Denny's in Annapolis, Maryland. I confessed to her how wrong I had been, I told her she wasn't crazy and that she had not done anything to deserve how terrible I had treated her. I told her I betrayed her trust over and over again and I was wrong. I turned her into a very bitter woman and she wasn't like that when we met. I asked her to forgive me, I told her if she didn't I'd understand but I wanted her to understand that this was my attempt to finally do the right thing by our son, by first attempting to get it right with his mother. Although humbling myself and admitting to my faults didn't guarantee that it would change anything, it was a start in the right direction. Fellas when you admit where and how you were wrong it releases you to change, and when you change people tend to change in response to you.

When I accepted my responsibility it made reconciliation possible. By reconciliation I mean to bring into agreement and to restore something back to a state of friendliness. That is what's needed if you're going to be able to have a positive influence. When I say bring into agreement I'm talking about joining your ideal world with reality or the world as it is.

For me I had to bring the ideal world (my son's

mother and I being able to raise him together) with my new reality (the fact that I'd screwed up the possibilities of being a full-time dad, and her now being his primary care provider and my being a part-time dad).

Now I can hear some of you guys saying "dude" you don't get it. My situation is different, you don't know her, she won't let go of the past, she left me, she is blocking me, she just took my kids and rolled out, she did this, and she did that. Trust me I get it. The bottom line is all of us have very different scenarios. I'm NOT proposing that there is a "One Size Fits All" solution here. I'm only suggesting that for the sake of your kids, do your very best to take your focus off of what you can't control. A much healthier alternative for everyone is to put your "energy" into what you can control, if for no other reason than to keep you from losing your mind. If there is one thing I do know, there are very few things that can compare to the pain of losing a child, whether you played a part in that or not. A loss is a loss. My goal is to help you keep your mind in the place of possibility. When your mind is focused on possibility there are options. Healthy options will appear. Truth is they've always been there but the pain and drama of focusing on that causes us to become blind to the healthy solution.

I had to accept that MY reality was that I may never get the opportunity to be a full time dad to my son. When I embraced that truth then the healthy options started becoming a little clearer. The first healthy option was the possibility of "Fathering from Afar". To be honest I didn't really like that idea but it was better than nothing. It began for me the journey of "Possibility". The next chapter will help you understand the importance of fighting to be involved, fully involved with raising your son and fathering from afar.

Chapter 5

Fathering From Afar

Don't allow distance (physical or emotional) to rob you of your relationship with your son.

This would be one of the most difficult challenges I'd face. Up until this point I'd never learned how to be a man. Let alone a father. All I knew was I didn't want for my son what I'd experienced growing up. In my book "How to Raise a Man …not a Mommas Boy!" I give a detailed description of how I felt as boy and what I experienced growing up without my dad. I won't go into that entire story, but for the sake of this chapter I would like to help you understand that my son's world had just been shattered. He was a toddler and had no clue that he was about to experience what it feels like to have a father that was "Missing in Action". I didn't have a dad to protect me or teach me how to protect myself. Consequently I got beat up a lot both literally and figuratively. I was bullied and picked on a whole lot. I remember as a kid being "afraid" to fight back so I would choose to run. It was terrible and still makes me angry to this day. Even today it is still a struggle to speak truth to myself, ask for help and saying YES when I want to say NO. My default is to run and hide and hope that it'll (whatever it is) just go away. I was left to figure it out all by myself and when that happens what's a boy to do? Glad you asked. I'll tell you. In most cases he makes very poor decisions unless he experiences the miracle of many strong, healthy, male influences, and he will wind up destroying himself and most of his relationships. It's not a matter of if, but when and how. The reality of your not being there for your child will cost more than any amount of money you can possibly pay.

Knowing this, my heart was overwhelmed with fear. This was a fear I had to face every single day that I was not with my son. My fear was fueled partly because I didn't know how to insure that growing up, with low or no self-esteem, a womanizing, sex crazed liar and cheater wouldn't be my son's fate. So based on what I had experienced from having a father that was uninvolved, I knew that if I wasn't involved that could possibly be his story. That's what motivated me to begin working on me. I knew I would have to raise my son from outside the house and that thought was scary as hell. I'd never seen it done successfully. I'm sure that there where those who'd done it, I'd just never seen it. This meant I was going to have to change, and become an unselfish person. I had to grow up and stop being what my first wife would have called "less of a man". I'll say upfront that this wasn't easy or an overnight process, for me it started with forcing myself to trust men. Then I had to put myself in a position to allow healthy men to mentor me, by making myself available to them. As I established a relationship with healthy brothers, I would have to open up and eventually tell my fears, my faults, and my desires to them. I'm so grateful to God that he had already started that process by allowing me to reconnect with a guy I knew named Deron Cloud. He was a real dude, who grew up in a crazy household. He was like me and many of the young boys who grew up in my neighborhood, who had been traumatized by what went on in life without understanding it and therefore the effects of the trauma went on undealt with.

We first met while I was a youth minister mentoring middle and high school students in the middle of my marital chaos. Another youth minister had encouraged me to bring him in to perform his one-man stage play for my youth group that he'd been touring locally to churches and community colleges in the area that dealt with boyfriend/girlfriend relationships. It was after seeing this very powerful production that I realized that we both had a desire to help youth. Before I knew it we had lost touch and I continued living my double life.

Little did I know that six years later while I was going through my separation that we would run into each other again nor did I know that my soon to be friend would play a key role in my being able to finally face myself. I was now working in radio and as I was sitting at my desk in walks Deron Cloud looking to do some advertising for his latest production. As we caught up on what we'd both been up to it became apparent that our lives had gone in different directions. His passion had transformed into his now being a pastor, and while my career in radio was growing my personal life was falling apart and I was consequently running from God. Over the next few months we would talk while working out at the gym and he would ask me some probing questions regarding my family. He was the first person to question my choices and it caused me to take a deeper look at myself. I didn't know it at the time but I was about to begin the journey to develop the qualities and character required to effectively "Father from Afar".

There were several qualities that I lacked in order to be a good father, some would take me years to gain but others were easier to gain once I committed to do what it took to father from afar. Learning to be accountable, walk in humility, being honest with others, and speaking truth to myself were key. This friendship with Deron was the first opportunity I had to see what accountability *Quality #1* meant and looked like and how it would be the basis of me changing me. The more we hung out the more I was able to let my guard down and open up about what I was really going through. He was the first person to ever challenge not only my actions but my way of thinking. He would ask me if I thought I was really being the kind of man that

I needed to be in order to raise a son, especially from afar. My character was severely damaged and to some extent was non-existent. I worked in an industry that paid me very well to lie and ruthlessly sell a service to people. As long as I got the job done I didn't have to be accountable to anyone, I could come and go as I pleased and do whatever I needed to do to get the deal done. I didn't know how nor did I have a desire to be accountable to anyone. However I knew that my lack of accountability was a result of my being left to myself and now it was a matter of pride and it was killing me and my chances of being a consistently adequate father.

It didn't happen overnight, it took me about three years before I would really embrace accountability and "get it". During that time I learned to humble myself *Quality #2*, be honest *Quality #3*, and speak truth to myself *Quality#4*. I read books suggested by my friend and I held myself accountable to a group of very positive men, who weren't perfect, which was great because neither was I, but they were committed to personal growth and with that came being honest with each other and sharing with each other, what was really going on. I shared stuff I hadn't told anybody. This was liberating for me and for the first time I felt like I could be me without being judged. This journey would be the beginning of me realizing that it was ok to be vulnerable. I will FOREVER be grateful to my friend, Deron Cloud for being the catalyst to push me toward growing up and become the man that I was designed to be. It was because of his relentless coaching that I had an example of what it looked to fight for what was most important.

If I was going to become a man that could be

trusted I had to do things that proved my trustworthiness, things like paying "child support". Dead beat dads don't get any respect, not because they don't care or are going through a "rough patch" but because when you decide to use that as an ***excuse*** not to take care of your child, nobody will respect you. If you're honest you don't respect yourself.

Notice I'm not dealing with how much money you should pay or time you should spend. I honestly believe that, that should be according to your ability to pay and spend time. Where it makes the mother angry and does the most damage to your child is when the father holds back or decides he just "ain't gonna" do anything to take care of his responsibilities. After all dude this child is your seed, a tiny particle of you. The question is do you want them to grow up properly? Who do you think is going to water the seed, nurture it and give it life? You are!! Don't take the way out that most of our fathers took and that was to let the boyfriend, the step-father, the streets, the school system, the government or their mother do what God designed you to do.

That's why it's vital, and a matter of life or death for your child, that you humble yourself and put up with whatever you have to take in order to have access in that child's life. Humility is the key. Even if the mother says screw you, if you do the right thing in time you will create a track record that overshadows the wrong you have done in the past. You hang in there no matter what, your seed needs you.

But You Don't Understand...

I'm fully aware that some of the women that you may deal with are plain crazy and unyielding. I also understand that no matter what you do to change; it may not mean anything to her. She very well may not budge and choose to remain bitter and vengeful. She's responsible for working on her or not. I know the horror stories of women who will use the child as a pawn just to spite the brother, but remember I said earlier. You can't change other people, you can only change you.

I asked my current wife who went through this with her daughter's father to share her thoughts on this subject and hear is a brief statement of what she told me ...

"Most women don't want to keep the father away from the child, they just want you to say you were wrong and ask for

her to forgive you. She wants to see you make every effort to be involved in the child's life, if it means seeing the child regularly or if you live in another state calling the child weekly just to say hi - not calling her trying to get back together but really pursuing a relationship with the child -- All women want a father for their children but it takes more than being a sperm donor or paying child support to be a father -- it takes work, it takes time, and it takes resources. When the mother is left to raise the child as the sole provider she needs to know that she is not alone and that she has your support in the decisions she makes for the child and that you are willing to help her."

It's for this reason that it's imperative that you work on your character, integrity and changing you by training yourself to take the high road. In the end what you sow you'll reap. It'll all come full circle. Always remember that **not being there for your child will cost more than any amount** *of money you can possibly pay*. On the other hand paying money only will never make up for your presence, influence, attention, touch, affirmation, correction, guidance, understanding, your ear, your heart, your empathy, or your conversation.

Give what you can, when you can as often as you can, time and treasure. Bottom line it takes a man to raise a man. You have to grow up and mature above the dumb stuff that doesn't matter. In the next chapter I share an interview with my first wife which allowed her to share her honest perspective.

Chapter 6

No More Baby Mama Drama

She wasn't bitter when you met her, if so you wouldn't have dealt with her. Eliminate the drama simply by showing her you care about your son.

In all honesty even though I did a bunch of work on myself to change so that I could give my son a fighting chance by becoming a model for him to follow, it was his mother changing that was the final key. I had dreamed of him one day coming to live with me but she never even considered it until she witnessed me changing. The opportunity for me to raise him came as a result of some changes his mother made as well. She came to several conclusions over the years that allowed her to make the decision to allow her only son to move to another state and be raised by his father. I would not be giving you a full picture of how much work it takes on both parts, if you didn't get to hear from her. I know that my situation doesn't fit everyone's but hopefully it will encourage you to move forward to do all you can do to fix yours. This is just the beginning. Here is the story that with God's help how a "woman scorned" was able to forgive and move on. She moved from bitter to better.

An interview with my first wife

Glenn: *I remember asking you, "Let me get him, I'd like to have a chance to raise him" Why did you say NO?*

First wife: *I recall YOU asking me to raise him once*

(maybe twice), although you have always emphasized that you were open to the idea, whenever I decided the time was right. On the other hand, I vividly remember him asking to go live with you several times, when he didn't want to comply with my requirements.

I said no based on my perception of your priorities and other observations. In the beginning, it did not appear that you were willing to focus your attention on his care full-time.

Glenn: I'd come to the conclusion that getting the opportunity to raise our son full time, for whatever reason would probably never happen. I pretty much gave up on the idea. Then one day you called me to talk about yet another incident that he'd been involved in school. Tell me how you were feeling that particular day?

First wife: That day, I was exhausted! I had begun to feel like I wasn't able to trust him. In fact, I had similar *feelings of disrespect, vulnerability and stress I felt when you and I were at the darkest times in our relationship. But, ironically, it was often your words that brought me clarity, when I would have to discipline him. I felt I had depleted my resources and as a last resort, I felt it was necessary to ask you to take your turn raising our son. I had talked to my husband about it, prayed about it and now, I really had peace about asking you. I knew I no longer had what he needed. I also knew that because your relationship with our son had become so established, there wasn't enough room or time, frankly, for my husband to cultivate the kind of relationship and respect necessary to turn him around. Don't get me wrong, they have their own kind of love relationship, but I believed his being with his own father, on a full-time basis, was what the doctor ordered. Consequently, when you agreed, it felt like a ton of weight was lifted off my shoulders.*

Glenn: *after hearing what he was doing, I simply said*

"You know him coming to live with me, isn't an option". Your response was WHY NOT? Why isn't it an option? Why did you challenge that statement?

First wife: *I challenged the statement because I felt strongly that it was your turn to sacrifice like I had for the first 13 years of his life. Now you were being offered an opportunity to do for your flesh and blood, what I had witnessed you do, from afar, with your daughter by marriage. I challenged you because I felt you owed him that much and should have jumped at the chance, at all costs.*

Glenn: *What was your mindset, regarding me raising our son, prior to that day in '07 versus your mindset today?*

First wife: *When we first separated, I remember having a conversation with you about refraining from dating when you had him for the weekend. I felt you had ample time between visits to do your single-thing and your time* with him should have been focused on developing a relationship with him. Furthermore, it was unacceptable for him to be telling me about visiting or spending the night over Ms. X's house, when he returned home. I also remember driving in the car and him piping up from the back seat, in his raspy little voice. He asked, "Mommy is it okay to be married and have a girlfriend too?" He was probably 4 or 5 years old. That floored me and I decided then that there had to be some major changes made before I would allow him to be subjected to such nonsense.

Glenn: What ultimately caused you to change your mindset and allow our son to come to Georgia, so that I could have an opportunity to raise him?

First wife: I guess the main cause is what I alluded to earlier—I knew he needed you! It's like my Uncle told me at one of our Father's Day gatherings. He said, "You don't *have what it takes to be mother and father to this boy." When I put all my personal criteria and apprehensions aside, I knew it was the right thing to do for him.*

There was a lot of work that went into her being able to come to this conclusion and allow her one and only child to move to another state to live with his father and step-mother. Over the years we had developed an excellent co-parenting relationship. My current wife and first wife would regularly discuss things regarding our son and we would come together to make decisions regarding his wellbeing. My current wife took an active role in our son's (yes I said our son, we don't ascribe to the whole step-parent thing) life, just as I had with our daughter (her daughter from a previous marriage). It was uncomfortable in the beginning and we made our share of mistakes but we all decided to put aside our personal feelings and do what was best for him. This show of unity is what eventually led to my first wife and her husband agreeing to let him come to live with me fulltime. I know that this is not normal and that in many cases it is hard enough for ex's to be civil let alone getting their respective new mates to go along with them being civil. If you make your child the priority and there are no ulterior motives for you being in communication with your ex then in time you can develop a co-parenting relationship that will allow you access to your child whether or not they ever come live with you.

Men if we are honest with ourselves we have a huge part that we play in most baby mama's drama. Most women are not mean and bitter when we hook up with them, if they were we would never get involved with them in the first place. Women become mean and bitter when they are repeatedly mistreated. Whether you were young and realized you weren't ready for a relationship after she got pregnant, you were married and were unfaithful, or you simply checked out of the relationship when you left and didn't fight for the relationship ... she was hurt. Very few women set out to get pregnant and raise a child on their own, they expect the father to be there and the fact that you aren't physically there is hurtful no matter what the reason. Be honest and admit where you were at fault to the mother of your child, humbly ask for her forgiveness over and over again, not because you want to get back with her but because you are truly sorry. Once you've apologized show her that your child is a priority in your life, show up when you say you will, do what you say you are going to do.

Whether you have the finances to pay child support or not should not prevent you from being a parent, if you have a good relationship with the mother she may show compassion if you are going through a rough patch financially, but if you don't talk and you never call your child she has no other choice than to take matters in to her own hands, or the hands of the courts to get what she can. This can open the door to your being able to play an active role in the life of your child without having to fight her every step of the way which can equal No Baby Mama Drama.

Chapter 7

Be Careful What You Ask For....

*What is the dog who is chasing the truck down the street going to do when he catches it?
That is the proverbial question.
The answer is found in preparation.*

The time had finally come and now it was my turn to sacrifice and do my part. This presented its own set of challenges. My wish was becoming a reality and now I was faced with what this would really cost me. This may sound crazy but after secretly praying for this day to come, when it had finally arrived my initial thought was "I can't afford this".

The moment came after I had made a career change and was not only working for a non-profit organization, but I had relocated to another state which had reduced our household income significantly. We were making it financially but there was little extra. On top of that my new wife and I were also enjoying the benefits of being "empty nesters". Our daughter was a senior in college living on her own and she had plans to go onto graduate school. Life was good initially I didn't see room to care for my son full time. Now I know how that sounds, but I'm being honest I was scared of just how this would play out. On top of that I really didn't think I had the energy to raise a 13 year old who was having problems with authority, struggling in school and needed my FULL attention.

All these thoughts went through my head when I heard the words on the phone that day "It's your turn". I knew in my heart that no matter how much I wanted to make excuses I was getting exactly what I asked for. I think there are times we ask for things not taking into account the cost involved, not only the physical but mental, emotional and even spiritual cost. It didn't take me long to make my decision and I am grateful for friends who not only told me the truth, but reminded me of what I had always wanted. One of my buddies encouraged me by saying "Hey…don't let your current financial situation determine whether or not you decide to take your son. Isn't this what you've always wanted? Well it's here brother, it's time to Man-Up". I had to admit that he was absolutely right and I had to do whatever to make this happen.

The timing will never be right, and you can always use the excuse that you aren't financially in a place to take on the responsibility, but the situation has never been perfect for her either but as a mother she just did what she had to do to make it happen. Remember at the end of the day you both created this child and he didn't ask to be here.

Once I wrapped my mind around the idea and accepting the possibility of my son being a FULL TIME part of my life I now had to discuss this with my wife. If I am honest I was not sure how she would respond. Don't get me wrong she loves my son and she had always been supportive but I wasn't sure how she would react. I remember sitting down and having the conversation with her and I'll never forget her response. "I'm fine with him coming, but". There it was the dreaded but, this is when I really got nervous. She proceeded to say "Your son needs you, he needs his father to step in and for the first time become his FULL time dad. That means YOUR time way more than our money. We'll figure the money part out, but you are going to have to prioritize your life so that it includes him in it FULL TIME. I am not going to become a single parent and raise him on my own, you have to be committed to being here!"

My wife knew that I had developed a pattern of putting work ahead of everything, even her at times and we had our share of challenges with my being "present". I loved doing what I did and helping people was my passion. My biggest problem was not putting up boundaries and being able to say no. I had a habit of saying yes to everything and everybody for the sake of "helping". What I know

now is that I got something out of helping people and I was fearful of letting people down because it made me feel good when I was pleasing others. My wife knew that if she didn't make this clear then I would agree to him coming to live with us but I would not make the commitment to be "present" so I could be there and do what needed to be done for my son.

We came to an agreement and put everything into motion. My son was coming to live with me FULL time for the first time at the age of 13. What I didn't know then was that the relationship that he and I had developed over the early years of his life from my getting him every other weekend and a few weeks in the summer was very different than the relationship that full time parents generally have with their kids.

It didn't dawn on me until he came to live with me how different our worlds where on a day to day basis. I got to see how he processed his thoughts and what he did and did not value. I began to understand why he was having so many problems at home and in school. He also got to see what my work week looked like. He saw what we valued and what we considered priority. It was really a culture shock that none of us had anticipated or expected. It was during this time that I also learned a whole lot about myself. Once again I was faced with the reality of how selfish I truly was. The honeymoon phase didn't last long and soon my wife was complaining about how my focus had returned to work and how I had slipped back into being ME focused again. My argument was she just didn't understand. I had adopted a "mission first, people always" mindset. That's a military term that really means do whatever you have to do in order to insure that the mission gets accomplished. Since we both are veterans I really didn't understand why she didn't get that. Well that's simple…the mission as far as the military is concerned is a matter of "National Defense" and if sacrificing people is what that takes then so be it. We've got a nation to be concerned about. My problem was that I took this motto way out of context. To my brothers like me that think what you do for a living is a matter of "National Defense" it's not. I would later come to the conclusion that my family particularly my seed and their wellbeing (physically, mentally, emotionally and spiritually) should be priority over my job, my hobbies, and what makes me feel good. Why? Because the people that matter most are the ones you bring into this world. The mission for a man should always be his family first. The job, friends, and others should always come after family. Even after my wife, very directly, reminded me of what the real mission should be, it still took me a while to "get it".

Men have been taught by the culture that we are supposed to provide for our families. However most of us have only seen that modeled from one perspective. That perspective being to go out earn a living and make sure that you do what you have to do to "feed" your family. That would be great if our families where only supposed to eat physically. The challenge comes when we find ourselves giving 70, 80 and over 90% of our time to that. What happens is that they starve mentally, emotionally and spiritually. I knew this on an intellectual level but had a very difficult time actually carrying this out on a day to day basis. I remember about a year after my son came to live with us in Georgia my wife had to have foot surgery. At the time things at work where ramping up for me. We were gearing up to take a stage play on tour, and I was in charge of promotions. I knew of my wife's upcoming surgery but instead of communicating with my colleagues the need to sit this one out. I came up with the idea of getting her girlfriend, who was unemployed at the time, to move into the house and take care of her and my son while I was on the road for three weeks. I can honestly say that although I had a job to do at work, my problem was that I loved what I did over who I was supposed to be to my family. My fear was, I can't afford that, what will my team think? I can't just leave them hanging. I honestly thought that replacing me with a willing, abled body and loving person in my wife's girlfriend, would be enough. I thought here is way to "kill two birds with one stone". Here was the problem…my wife and my son **needed me.** They say that "hind sight is 20/20", if that's true then please be willing to see your situation through the lens of my mistakes. I wasn't being considerate of what my wife and son thought or felt. I ignored them when they both had been saying prior to this situation that "you're not here", "you're not present", "even when you are here you're always working in your office and you're not here". **Here is a tip guys**, when those closest to you have a problem with how you are treating them. Chances are you need to figure out what you are doing or not doing that creates and environment that would allow them to feel that way. It's you not them, if I were a betting man, I'd put money on it.

The biggest lesson that I've learned now that my kids are grown… **"LISTEN twice as much as you talk"**. That's why we have two … count them two ears and one mouth. My son was telling me in his acting out, fighting, disrespecting authority, not turning in his school work. Dad *I NEED* you to be here. You see I had this foolish thought that said, I am here. We did stuff together when I wasn't working and his needs were provided for, I mean he had his own room, food to eat and clothes. I believed the selfish lie that I was doing my best. Not so, said my reality. My wife was bothered with me because once again my son was being raised by a woman. Not a man, not his father.

After being on the road for three weeks after my wife's foot surgery I began to take a hard look at myself and did some serious soul searching. We got a family counselor that came to the house once a week almost for the remainder of the school year. Over the course of those next six months I did work on me. Although I had experienced challenges with raising my daughter almost eight years prior. My son was a different breed. He was a boy that was left to himself with an overworked mom and a part time dad. He had problems. I learned in counseling that he was still angry because of his mom and me splitting up although it had been over ten years ago at that time. He was mourning the loss of his friends and family in Maryland and although he wanted to come live with me, he was still sad. I didn't understand that this kind of abrupt separation could take a couple years to get completely over even if handled properly. It was more than a thing he could just "walk off", "snap out of" or the famous "just get it together man".

GLENN P. BROOKS, JR.

Chapter 8

Mending Broken Pieces

Even when the relationship is shattered, it is still possible to put it back together. It's going to be hard work but your son is worth it.

Although I'd gotten my son back physically, he was broken. He was broken emotionally and it was my job to see that he was put back together. That took me to humble myself on a regular basis and not blame him for just being un-manageable. I never will forget when our family counselor, told me you're son **needs you.** He actually wants to please you but the problem is because of the way his brain works he can't logically connect the dots to do that. His relationship with you is a "give to get" type thing, he thinks that ***he can't get love until he gives compliance.*** She taught me how to work on that with what she called the 30 minute rule. Our assignment was to spend 30 minutes a day together at least 3 times a week - just us time. During this time I was not allowed to coach, instruct, teach a lesson or fix anything. We had to just be with each other spending time. We would have to agree on what we would do and do it together. This helped us to develop a new relationship based on love and not based on meeting an expectation. We played chess and just loved on each other no matter what problems we were having, in school, at work, or anywhere else for that matter. It was during that time that I recognized that his problems largely were created by me or should I say the absence of me.

During my time as a part time dad we had to hold

him back in school due to his having some academic challenges which stemmed from his behavioral issues. Then the year he moved to Georgia he failed his first year of school living with me as a result of his transitioning and adapting to a new school and home. I think his academic challenges were a result of unhealed emotional wounds which showed up as behavioral issues. Everyone was focused solely on his behavior and as a result he wasn't getting what he needed in order to achieve his academic goals. When the father is active and present in a child's life it's very tough for the child to slip through the cracks. Think about it, men are typically bottom line oriented, as soon as we smell that there is a problem most of us shift our minds to "how am I going to fix this". That's why we are depended on for leadership and direction. When we are out of position, everyone suffers, especially our children. My truth is that like my father left me to myself for much of my son's life I did the same thing to him. The only way we break this cycle is through love. Loving ourselves enough to be brutally honest with where we are messing up. Loving our children's mother enough to look past her faults and see her need for a loving leader and loving our children enough not to quit on them. My son's middle school and high school years were very challenging, he and I were learning how to be father and son while he was processing through his emotional trauma. I am grateful for the opportunity to see firsthand how he grew from a child to a young man. Watching him try different things in an effort to find his niche, from playing basketball, to wanting to be a chef, to writing and producing rap music. It was a pleasure to watch him evolve. While I was finally starting to figure this thing out, he was coming to some conclusions on his own. All children have a mind of their own and no matter how much you want them to do something there comes a time in their life when they begin to make choices based on what they want or don't want to do. This can be disheartening for some and it can be refreshing for others. Their ability to make choices on their own is a part of their development and it can be hard to sit by and watch your child make self- destructive choices. Every parent wants the best for their child, you want them to succeed in life, but I had to learn the hard way that I can not want his success more than he wanted it for himself. A father's job is to train, instruct, motivate, and guide our children in the direction for success, but they have to be in agreement. When children are in elementary and even in middle school we can pretty much make them do what we want them to do, but by the time they reach high school things change. At some point in their life every child will make a bad choice, this does not make them bad it is simply a lack of good judgment at that moment. As difficult as it may be to watch them make bad choices it is far worse to cut them off and not remain available as a support for them. My son and I had our share of heated disagreements regarding some of the choices he was making, but I loved him through all of it. He eventually made some really poor choices which led to his dropping out of school and leaving our home. He left the nest far sooner than I would have liked but life has its way of teaching us all how to make wiser choices.

The first year after him leaving home was one of the roughest patches we have gone through in our relationship and at the time I feared I had lost him once again. I remember that it was one of the most painful things I had to go through. Nobody wants to see their child struggle especially when he or she hasn't been fully equipped. My truth was that I missed out on the opportunity to train him in certain areas and part of what he was going through was a direct result of a "lack of training".

He went through a period of almost two years trying to figure it out. It was during this time while he was at Job Corps that by his admission he was able to articulate that now he understood why I was so hard on him about the basics of studying hard and taking advantage of every opportunity that presents itself. He went on to tell me that if it wasn't for the education that he had received after moving to Georgia that he would not have been able to pass his GED exam on his first attempt. Although our relationship had changed during this time, it made me understand the value of stepping back and allowing him to work through his own situation. I often feel like I was robbed of the opportunity to teach him all that he needed to know. It was during this time that I had a flash back moment. My son shared with me the same thing my daughter had said when she was about to go off to college. He said "Dad I still need you". It's a sobering and humbling thing when your soon to be grown children sit down with you and say that although they are no longer children, they still need you. I, like many parents believed the foolish notion that "my job" was to get them to 18 and the rest was up to them. That just isn't true. They may not need you as the "Parent" but they certainly need you as "Coach" Dad.

Today I have a great and constantly growing relationship with my son. He calls me on a regular basis to share with me what he's thinking and to seek wisdom on how to process through his thoughts. I love our adult relationship and my hope is that you can learn from my mistakes and get your son back as well. No matter what phase of life your son is in, whether he's a toddler, in elementary or high school it's never too late. Make an effort to establish a relationship with your son. Every boy needs their father, if for no other reason than to gain an understanding of where he comes from. You may not have been the best father in the past or you may have allowed the loss of your relationship with his mother to cause you to pull back but the fact remains your son needs you. Only a father can give their son the love of a father, there is something beautiful and rewarding about having a real relationship with your seed. He is your contribution to this world and don't you want to have a hand in shaping him into the man he can be? No matter how uncomfortable it may be dealing with his mom, no matter how many miles separate you the cost of not being there is far too high to not do all you can to get your son back.

Final Thoughts

All children deserve to have both of their parents in their lives, whether you are together or not. Boys need their fathers to teach them how to become men; just as much as girls need their fathers to teach them how to value themselves and what to look for in a man.

There is a crisis in our nation when one out of every three children is being raised without their father - but this can change one father at a time. Men take a stand and BE the father you always wanted and needed to your children.

GLENN P. BROOKS, JR.

ABOUT THE AUTHOR
GLENN P. BROOKS, JR.

Born in South Baltimore Maryland where he was raised by a single mother after his parents divorced. Although he experienced a great deal of trauma in his life as a child, Glenn always seemed to have a magnetic personality that made it very easy to capture the attention of others.

After High School he joined the Army and served as a Combat Engineer, this experience served as his introduction to the world of leadership. During his military service, Glenn later began serving the youth of his local church and there found one of his many passions, which was to make a difference in the lives of children. As a youth worker Glenn has touched hundreds of students' lives over the last 25 years.

After his military service he went into the broadcasting industry where he continued to grow as a leader, working as an intern, on-air announcer, Program Director, and Station Manager. Glenn continues his work in broadcasting as a voice talent and media consultant. He also has been able to continue to fulfill his passion to make a difference in the lives of children and families through his work as a mentor, speaker, and relationship coach.

Today he works with various school systems, human service agencies, and ministries doing what he does best, which is inspiring, motivating, teaching, training and ultimately leading others to understand, that it's not where a man starts that matters, it's where he finishes that counts.

Glenn and his wife Sheri are the founders of Constant Relationship Coaching and are the proud parents of two children. They currently reside in the Atlanta, Georgia metropolitan area.

GLENN P. BROOKS, JR.

Visit www.thecrcoach.com

For booking information and services offered by
Constant Relationship Coaching

Check out these titles by the author
Available on Amazon.com

How To Raise A Man…Not A Momma's Boy!
By Glenn P. Brooks, Jr.

Living With A Momma's Boy
A guide to understanding and dealing with the momma's boy
in your life without losing your mind
By Sheri A. Brooks and Glenn P. Brooks, Jr.

Made in the USA
Middletown, DE
20 January 2016